ESTHER RANTZEN'S
CHILDLINE
CHRISTMAS BOOK

DRAGON
An imprint of the Children's Division
of the Collins Publishing Group
8 Grafton Street, London W1X 3LA

Published by Dragon Books 1987

ISBN 0 583 31229 2

Printed and bound in Great Britain by
Collins, Glasgow

Dear Reader

CHRISTMAS IS, OF COURSE, A VERY SPECIAL TIME FOR CHILDREN. FOR LOVED CHILDREN IT IS USUALLY THE BEST SEASON OF THE YEAR, WITH TREATS AND PRESENTS AND FAMILIES GATHERED TOGETHER IN JOY. BUT FOR UNLOVED CHILDREN, THE THOUSANDS OF CHILDREN WHO ARE NEGLECTED OR ABUSED, CHRISTMAS CAN BE ESPECIALLY PAINFUL. THE BRILLIANT CHRISTMAS LIGHTS ONLY HIGHLIGHT THEIR LONELINESS. ONE LITTLE GIRL TOLD ME IN A LETTER – "ONE CHRISTMAS MY PARENTS DIDN'T BUY ME ANYTHING, AND FOR SOME REASON THEY SAID I WASN'T ALLOWED ANY DINNER. I REMEMBER CRYING ON MY OWN. BUT THEN THE LITTLE GIRL NEXT DOOR SAID I COULD PLAY WITH HER, SHE MUST HAVE TOLD HER MUM BECAUSE SHE DISAPPEARED INTO HER KITCHEN AND CAME BACK WITH A HOT CHRISTMAS DINNER FOR ME, TURKEY AND ALL THE TRIMMINGS. IT WAS THE BEST MEAL I EVER HAD – AND HER WHOLE FAMILY TALKED SO KINDLY TO ME INSTEAD OF THE ANGRY SHOUTS I WAS USED TO. THAT IS THE ONLY HAPPY MEMORY OF MY CHILDHOOD."

WHEN WE FIRST INVENTED CHILDLINE, SO THAT UNHAPPY CHILDREN COULD RING 0800-1111 AND TALK ABOUT THEIR PAIN TO A COUNSELLOR WHO OFFERS COMFORT AND HELP, WE BELIEVED THAT CHRISTMAS WOULD BE A SPECIAL TIME FOR CHILDLINE TOO. SO WE WROTE TO A MULTITUDE OF CARING PEOPLE IN SHOW BUSINESS, IN POLITICS, IN THE ARTS, IN SPORT, ASKING IF THEY WOULD HELP US BY SENDING A CHRISTMAS CARD TO CHILDLINE. THE LOVELY, AMUSING, TOUCHING CARDS YOU WILL FIND IN THIS BOOK WERE THEIR ANSWER. WE WOULD LIKE TO THANK THEM ALL.

WE MUST ALSO THANK SARAH CAPLIN AND HER TEAM AT "CHILDWATCH", AND ADRIAN SINGTON AND HIS TEAM AT COLLINS FOR MAKING OUR DREAM COME TRUE AND THIS BOOK BECOME A REALITY. THE PROFITS FROM IT WILL PAY FOR THE PHONE CALLS CHILDREN MAKE TO CHILDLINE – THE MORE WE SELL THE MORE NEW PHONE LINES CAN BE OPENED. AT THE MOMENT WE ARE TAKING A THOUSAND CALLS A DAY BUT MANY MORE THOUSANDS OF CHILDREN STILL CAN'T GET THROUGH. WE LONG TO BE ABLE TO HELP THESE CHILDREN TOO.

A LETTER I WILL NEVER FORGET WAS SENT TO ME BY A YOUNG WOMAN – SHE SAID "ALL MY CHILDHOOD I WAS ABUSED BUT I KEPT IT SECRET. I WAS SILENCED BY FEAR – SCREAMING ON THE INSIDE, BUT NOTHING CAME OUT. I ACHE WHEN I THINK THAT SO MANY CHILDREN ARE STILL SUFFERING AS I DID. PLEASE HELP TO CREATE A PLACE WHERE CHILDREN CAN BE LISTENED TO AND BELIEVED."

CHILDLINE IS THAT PLACE. THE DEDICATED TEAM THERE WORK EVERY DAY TO HELP PROTECT AND COMFORT CHILDREN – BY BUYING THIS BOOK YOU WILL ALLOW THEM TO HELP EVEN MORE CHILDREN. AND WE HOPE IT WILL ALSO BRING YOU A GREAT DEAL OF PLEASURE TO READ, THIS CHRISTMAS.

WITH LOVE,

Esther Rantzen

merry christmas
from the children of
Child Line!

ESTHER RANTZEN

BUCKINGHAM PALACE

HRH PRINCE EDWARD PASSES HIS BEST WISHES TO EVERYONE INVOLVED WITH CHILDLINE FOR THE VERY WORTHWHILE WORK THAT THEY DO.

THE DUKE AND DUCHESS OF YORK SEND EVERYONE AT CHILDLINE THEIR BEST WISHES FOR CHRISTMAS AND EVERY GOOD WISH FOR YOUR FUTURE ENDEAVOURS.

THE ARCHBISHOP OF CANTERBURY OFFERS HIS PRAYERS AND BEST WISHES FOR THE VERY IMPORTANT WORK DONE BY CHILDLINE.

THANK YOU FOR YOUR WONDERFUL WORK. WE MUST ALL HELP. LOVE TO ALL CHILDREN.

MARGARET THATCHER

PETER BLAKE

The best bit is early in the morning, when the family joins in my youngest daughter's excitement in opening her presents. It's a high tech time, with mountains of glossy paper revealing batteries, silicon chips carolling, and things made exquisitely in amazing plastics.

In the corner, a television set waits to do its party piece.

Then, we find a Rupert book, and at once, it takes me back to another Rupert book, in a pillow case, at the bottom of an old fashioned bed. There's a Meccano set, and the paper decorations my mother made. There's a pudding with silver

TONY ROSS

threepenny pieces in it, and as my father sits in his chair by the radio, his hand smoothes the brand new scarf on his lap, remembering when…

Uncle Sid has given Kate a "Pooh" video, my wife clicks it into the machine, we go to see to the lunch, and the Christmas giggles are just the same.

TONY ROSS

DEAR CHILDLINE, A VERY HAPPY CHRISTMAS.

I'm working, as usual at this time of year at Ronnie Scott's Jazz Club. We 'break up' on the 23rd and so, early on Christmas Eve, I catch a train for Wales and the Tower we have there. We spend a restful three days there with lots to eat and drink. Diana, my wife, cooks delicious meals. My son Tom and step-daughter Candy are there. Everything glows and sparkles. Come the 27th it's back to the stuffy night-club.

GEORGE MELLY

HAVE A BRILL YULETIDE

SANTA LOOKS AFTER THEM

ONE DAY A YEAR.

LET US LOOK AFTER THEM

THE OTHER 364.

My Christmas Day will

be spent at home and I'll

spare a thought for those

alone. If I had a

Christmas wish it would

be that every family will

live together happily.

SYD LITTLE AND EDDIE LARGE

LITTLE AND LARGE

And three astrologers came from the East to worship the Lord, they had seen his star rise and followed it to the place where he was born.

RUSSELL GRANT

RUSSELL GRANT

PEACE ON EARTH – GOOD WILL, KINDNESS AND TOLERANCE TO ALL MEN.

Love

RUSSELL GRANT

P.S. KEEP UP YOUR MARVELLOUS WORK.

WE ALWAYS HAVE A GREAT FAMILY CHRISTMAS. WE WISH ALL CHILDREN COULD HAVE THE SAME.

Our Christmas is a Dickensian one with games and get togethers, and visits to relatives. We usually sit down twenty strong (or fairly strong!) at Christmas Dinner, and then we all play Wink Murder over the coffee! Twenty cards – one each – one is the Ace of Spades – whoever gets that is the murderer, and has to wink at each person in turn without being detected by the others. The winkee counts to 5 (under the breath) and then dies in as hammy a way as possible. The winning murderer is the one who claims the most victims!! With love from all of us.

Merry Christmas!! xxxxxx. Leslie Crowther

LESLIE CROWTHER

LESLIE CROWTHER

ROD CAMPBELL

To Childline to wish you a merry Christmas and a happy New Year

We'll all be up about 5.30. Down to the Serpentine for a wake-up dip. Then family judo to warm us up for breakfast at 6.45. Then prayers and television till 2.00pm. Then we distribute presents among the needy in Holland Park. 2.02pm Xmas lunch with break for Queen's Message 11.30pm, finish lunch. Post prandial nap and up-chucking. Wake up about 4.00pm on 28th.

JOHN CLEESE

P.S. Sorry about the card but design is not my strongest facet. In fact, I am absolutely bloody terrible!

ERNIE WISE

Christmas bells ring out across the Christmas snow carols are sung, holly is hung Christmas cards come and go To the children of Childline I bring you sunshine and love

ERNIE WISE

Love, light and peace

SPIKE MILLIGAN

BEST WISHES

To Childline from

NORMAN TEBBIT

FAITH BROWN

I am looking forward to Christmas. This is the time of year I like best of all. I make sure I am with my family. My daughter, Danielle will be 10 on the 10th December. She looks forward to it because Christmas is just around the corner and she gets excited because she knows her Gran and relations will be coming to stay with us.

FAITH BROWN

TRACEY ULLMAN

MERRY CHRISTMAS FROM SOMEONE WHO CAN'T DRAW. HAVE A COOL YULE. IT BREAKS MY HEART TO THINK OF UNHAPPY CHILDREN. BECOMING A PARENT MYSELF PUTS SO MUCH IN PERSPECTIVE. GOOD LUCK AND BEST WISHES.

XXXX
TRACEY ULLMAN

TRACEY ULLMAN

happy
christmas
from the three
wise bears

a fifi original
by
Fiona Richmond

FIONA RICHMOND

HAPPY CHRISTMAS FROM THE THREE WISE BEARS

My daughter, Tara will be two, three days after Christmas. She loves pigs and we live very near to the New Forest. So I expect to spend a lot of time looking at very fat and very dirty pigs with her.

Lots of love,

FIONA RICHMOND

MERRY CHRISTMAS

On Christmas Day I hope to be doing a lot of flopping around on sofas, reeking of new perfume with chocolate round my mouth. I will be pursuing my husband round the house with a new sweater which he will not want to wear because it is grey and might draw attention to him.

Love

Victoria Wood

VICTORIA WOOD

VICTORIA WOOD

DAVID SHILLING

I AM DELIGHTED TO BE ABLE TO DO SOMETHING TO HELP CHILDLINE.

I shall spend most of Christmas morning in the Cathedral – then after lunch with the Cathedral Clergy, I shall be giving out presents to our Choristers (they go home in the afternoon). I shall then go to visit some people who will not have too much to make Christmas a happy one – when I return to Archbishop's House, I'll put my feet up! With all good wishes for Christmas and the New Year.

BASIL HUME, ARCHBISHOP OF WESTMINSTER

P.S, I AM NOT ABLE TO DESIGN A CARD – I SIMPLY WOULD NOT KNOW HOW TO GO ABOUT IT.

DAVID SHILLING

My selection box for Christmas Day excludes politics, politicians and problems. It includes family, friends and children – and more turkey and Xmas pudding than is good for us.

Every good wish

RT. HON. JACK ASHLEY C.H., M.P.

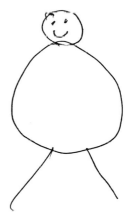

A Silly Chistmas Card.

ALEXEI SAYLE

❦❦ MERRY CHRISTMAS AND A
HAPPY NEW YEAR
*I will spend Christmas
Day with my family.
It will be a good day
this year as Daniel is
4 and Samuel will be
15 months.
Hilary and I have lunch
at her or my parents on
alternative years, then all
my relations and hers
come back to our house
in the evening to have a
family party.
We are lucky that all our
family are close and we
enjoy a family day.
Best wishes* ❦❦

BILL BEAUMONT

❦❦ HAVE A VERY SILLY
CHRISTMAS ❦❦

ALEXEI SAYLE

BILL BEAUMONT

God bless and fondest
love to Childline

Last year our Christmas
Day was very unusual –
as we were in Australia –
we still had a tree and
traditional decorations
but as it was very hot we
had cold *roast turkey and*
Santa Claus visited us
in shorts!

Love and best wishes

RULA LENSKA AND
DENNIS WATERMAN

RULA LENSKA AND
DENNIS WATERMAN

RONNIE BARKER

A very merry Christmas

RONNIE BARKER

LJILJANA RYLANDS

❦❦ To Childline, Season's Greetings My Love and Best Wishes Always.

I'm looking forward to a quiet family Christmas, with my wife, my two sons and their girl friends. Traditional Christmas lunch, perhaps a game of Trivial Pursuits, and a snooze…!! I'm afraid I couldn't begin to design a Christmas card! I couldn't even draw matchstick men for my sons when they were little! Sorry! love ❦❦

GORDON JACKSON

ANGELA DOUGLAS

BOB WILSON

❦❦ Herewith the message. Sorry I'm hopeless at art – the card must be by-passed

Christmas for me means family. It also means the love and joy of children. I always attend Church on Christmas Day and that is important – but in the end the sheer joy of children not only in receiving but also in giving – is pure magic. I love the carols too – not to mention all that lovely food!!! ❦❦

from

CYRIL SMITH M.B.E., M.P.

GOD IS LOVE,

AND LOVE IS ALL.

IN EVERY SPECK OF SNOW,

A MILLION KISSES FALL.

WITH HAPPINESS, HAPPINESS

IN CHRISTMAS, NEW YEAR

AND ALL.

Christmas Day is the one day of the year I can really let go and enjoy myself. I spend it with the people I love.

My husband, dad, mum and mum-in-law and sister-in-law.

We open presents together, eat together and enjoy each other's company. Catch up on the year's gossip.

I love Christmas, because I love to give, especially the unexpected. I find out what each person has

secretly wished for that year and make sure they get it. I find this more fun than receiving presents. Christmas has always been the one time I feel secure.

love

TOYAH WILCOX

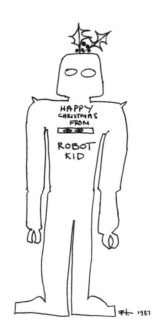

PETE TOWNSHEND

My Dad made me a Robot to live in. It doesn't need a phone — hope you never need yours (It's a bit lonely in here, but

IT'S SAFE!)

childline — for kids without robots.

0800 - 1111

PETE TOWNSHEND

"MERRY CHRIMBLE TO YE!"

PAUL McCARTNEY

All the best to kids everywhere!

love
Paul McCartney

PAUL McCARTNEY

 DRAWING IS NOT MY STRONG

SUIT – I COULD STAND A

REJECTION!

HAPPY CHRISTMAS.

CHILDLINE (CHILDLIKE!)

SNOWMAN – WITH PHONE

NUMBER

MICHAEL GRADE

'CHILDLINE (CHILDLIKE!) SNOWMAN – WITH PHONE NUMBER'

MICHAEL GRADE

BABETTE COLE

I HOPE YOU LIKE THIS CARD. IT'S A PICTURE OF ME AND MY ENTIRE FAMILY SHOOTING DOWN THE HILLY HILLS OF ELHAM.

love
Babette

BABETTE COLE

I AM DELIGHTED TO SEND A MESSAGE OF GOOD WISHES TO CHILDLINE AND AM SURE THAT, THROUGH YOUR EFFORTS, MANY CHILDREN WILL SPEND A HAPPIER CHRISTMAS. IN THE METROPOLITAN POLICE WE SUPPORT YOUR EFFORTS AND WILL ALWAYS HELP IN THE CARE OF CHILDREN IN TROUBLE OR DANGER. YOU WILL BE IN MY THOUGHTS AT HOME ON CHRISTMAS DAY.

SIR KENNETH NEWMAN

Christmas starts for us as usual, feeding, watering and walking the animals – 2 dogs and 3 cats – who know it's Christmas 'cos of the smell of turkey coming from the larder. We open family presents at 12 noon and then start preparations for the meal. People arrive about 4 for Tea and Christmas Cake – which I make in September – then presents and stockings and we sit down to 'The Meal' at 7ish – so most of my Christmas Day is spent in the kitchen – I love it!

PENELOPE KEITH

P.S. SORRY NO DESIGN FOR A CARD – FOR A GOOD COOK I'M A LOUSY DRAWER!!

I cannot draw

but wish genuine happiness to all children

David Steel

THE RT. HON. DAVID STEEL M.P.

TO ALL THE YOUNGSTERS, WITH EVERY BLESSING TO YOU, AND MAY 1988 BE SO GOOD TO YOU.

From: Henry Cooper & family.

HENRY COOPER

HELEN OXENBURY

QUENTIN BLAKE

THE FOLLOWING TWELVE CARDS HAVE BEEN DRAWN SPECIALLY FOR CHILDLINE BY SOME OF BRITAIN'S LEADING CHILDREN'S ILLUSTRATORS AND HAVE BEEN REPRODUCED BY KIND PERMISSION OF GORDON FRAZER LTD. THEY CAN BE BOUGHT IN THE SHOPS THIS CHRISTMAS.

LEON BAXTER

JOHN BURNINGHAM

MICHAEL FOREMAN

ROY GERRARD

NICOLA BAYLEY

DAVID McKEE

MICK INKPEN

ANTONY BROWN

JILL BARKLEM

NICK BUTTERWORTH

🎄 *Christmas Day for me is, I imagine, like Christmas Day for many people, a family occasion, with our sons and their girls, and always a friend or two who spend the Christmas holiday with us. There are carols and the presents under the tree, opening these takes most of the morning. Then, of course, Christmas Dinner – followed by listening to the Queen's speech and a lethargic afternoon, before we liven up for games and jollity in the evening. All very simple, but I wish that everyone was able to enjoy the same tranquillity and togetherness.* 🎄

*with love from
Mollie Sugden*

MOLLIE SUGDEN

BERNIE WINTERS

MOLLIE SUGDEN

🎄 BEST WISHES FOR CHRISTMAS AND THE NEW YEAR

I shall be spending a quiet Christmas this year surrounded by my favourite girls – Siggi my wife, Schnorbitz, Ella and Putzi my three dogs, and of course the mother-in-law! Keep up the good work 🎄

Love
Bernie Winters

BERNIE WINTERS

❦ To Childline

We love you.

All my love to

Childline. (My heart is

in the right place even

if my pen isn't!)

I don't spend a very

'clever' day. I go off my

diet! Force the cocker

spaniel to walk miles

after lunch to <u>run my</u> fat

off. Try – and fail – to

play my 15 year-old son

Gresby's 'electrical'

presents (video games

etc). Pull crackers. Crack

nuts and awful jokes!

Grumble about

<u>everything</u> on TV – but

still watch it. COOK!

EAT! and EAT! Admire

my Mum, husband and

son for not being as

'Piggy' as I am! Roll into

bed like a BARREL! ❦

Love

JEAN ROOK

JEAN ROOK

JIMMY TARBUCK

❦ I wish you all a smile at

Christmas, and to every

child in the world

happiness ❦

love

JIMMY TARBUCK

TWIGGY BY BARBARA HULANICKI

MERRY CHRISTMAS

Jan Twiggy
xxx

TWIGGY

PHOTOGRAPHY BY

BARBARA HULANICKI

COSTUME BY MARCUS

ERSKINE-PULLEN WITH HELP

FROM NOLI

MAKE-UP BY MARY LYNDON

WITH THANKS

TO ALL THE HARDWORKING

TEAM AT CHILDLINE AND

ALL THE DEPRIVED

CHILDREN THROUGHOUT THE

BRITISH ISLES. HOPING YOU

HAVE A VERY MERRY

CHRISTMAS AND A HAPPY

PEACEFUL NEW YEAR.

THINKING OF YOU NOW AND

ALWAYS.

LOTS OF LOVE.

BARRY McGUIGAN

THIS IS TO WISH YOU AND

EVERYBODY AT CHILDLINE A

GOOD AND PEACEFUL

CHRISTMAS

I will be with my children

– all three of them are

quite big now – but we

will use the time to enjoy

being together and

sharing the different

Xmas rituals. We will not

forget children whose

lives are bare and empty

but will rejoice that you

are helping so many of

them.

Love

LADY JANE EWART-BIGGS

CONGRATULATIONS ON THIS

PROJECT AND ITS MASSIVE

RESPONSE.

CHEERS!

ALAN FREEMAN

FELIX BOWNESS AND
FRED QUILLY OF HI-DE-HI.

No child really needs gold frankincense or myrrh. All it really needs is Love.

DAVID KOSSOFF

No child really needs gold, frankincense or myrrh.

All it really needs is love.

Give a child a happy Xmas. Give it love

We admire very much your hard work. It is hard work. Not to prompt the call from the child, but to get a name, a clue, a way to really help. Who can fight fear? So our thoughts this Xmas will be with you all – and with all the children making up their minds to phone you.

DAVID & JENNIE KOSSOFF

Happy Christmas to children everywhere

I hope to spend Christmas with my son and his family, including our two teenage grandchildren. Their Grampy and I always have a lovely time with them – they won't let us help with the washing-up!

MARJORIE PROOPS

MARJE PROOPS

TO ALL AT...

Childline

with love from

Nick Ross

NICK ROSS

Well I still think he looks Jewish

NICK ROSS

🍃🍃 HAVE A BEAUTIFUL XMAS
AND A WONDERFUL NEW
YEAR

*This year I'll be spending
my Xmas Day next to an
open fire in a cottage
nestled in the Yorkshire
Dales. It may even be a
white one but for sure
there'll be lots of fun
and family and too
much food!
To everyone at Childline,
have a lovely Xmas and
a special New Year.* 🍃🍃

SHARRON DAVIES

*To Wish You
a Very
Merry Christmas.*

SHARRON DAVIES

PATRICK HUGHES

I am not going to spend my Christmas this year. To make up for some of the Christmases I have mis-spent in the past, I am going to save this one up to add to some of the Christmases to come to make them fuller and thicker.

Patrick Hughes

PATRICK HUGHES

STAN HAYWARD AND
BOB GODFREY

WISHING YOU A MERRY CHRISTMAS AND HAPPY LANDINGS IN THE NEW YEAR.
I shall be spending Christmas Day with my family and four young nieces – having a real "family party" – Best wishes to everyone!

With love Bonnie xx

BONNIE LANGFORD

Last Christmas I spent in a supine position, as I had just two days off from "Wonderful Town", which was playing in the West End. I had seen so little of my own kids during the previous few months that I really just wanted to watch them unwrapping and fighting – and giving cheek for hours on end.
My parents from Hull were with us, and we had a Christmas dinner and some friends over in the afternoon for a sing around the out-of-tune piano.
Boxing Day – two shows and its Chanukah – 1st day of lighting the candles for the Festival of Light. A happy time.

love Maureen x

MAUREEN LIPMANN

❦❦ BEST WISHES TO
CHILDLINE. WE HOPE THIS
CARD HELPS TOWARDS
RAISING FUNDS FOR A VERY
WORTHWHILE CAMPAIGN. **❦❦**
PRINCESS MICHAEL OF KENT

❦❦ *I hope to spend*
Christmas wrapping and
unwrapping presents.
I hope to sing carols and
wake up with a stocking

I hope to spend christmas wrapping and
unwrapping presents. I hope to sing carols and wake up with a stocking at my feet.
Eating turkey and playing with toys and
spending time with my family.
With best wishes Frederick Windsor.

LORD FREDERICK WINDSOR

at my feet. Eating turkey
and playing with toys
and spending time with
my family. **❦❦**

With best wishes Frederick Windsor

LORD FREDERICK WINDSOR

❦❦ P.S. THE RED SPOT ON THE
RIGHT HAND SIDE OF MY
PICTURE IS RUDOLPH'S NOSE. **❦❦**

JAN LEEMING

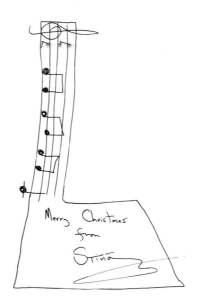

STING

 PEACE AND JOY AT CHRISTMAS

Last Christmas was un-typical because I was working at BBC Television Centre on both Christmas and Boxing Day. That was my ninth and last 'working' Christmas. We had presents and lunch before I left for work on Christmas Day – the rest of which was spent reading the news and praying that there would be no disasters!

JAN LEEMING

 MERRY CHRISTMAS

STING

RAYMOND BRIGGS

CAROL LAWSON

CHRIS McEWAN

❦ HAPPY CHRISTMAS…
AND NEW YEAR
*My Christmas day will be
a family day – my own
family – which includes
Daniel and Jake my
teenage sons – my
parents, my husband's
mother, and possibly
seven extras – brothers,
nieces, nephews, plus at
least four dogs and one
cat called Alice.
We will go to Church,
then give each other
presents, before enjoying
a traditional lunch.
Friends will arrive,
and their children will
be given presents off
our tree.
In short – our Christmas
Day is about family,
friendship and love.* ❦

Judith Hann

JUDITH HANN

CLIFF RICHARD

JUDITH HANN

❦ BETTER A
CHRISTMAS/SACRED
THAN CHRIST/MASSACRED.
HAVE A PEACE-FILLED TIME!
*I'm looking forward to a
happy family Christmas
– here's hoping you all
have a wonderful time.* ❦

Luv!

Cliff Richard

CLIFF RICHARD

ROLF HARRIS

❦❦ HAPPY CHRISTMAS AND A
PROSPEROUS NEW YEAR
Hopefully we will have a
lovely lazy family day at
home with everyone
waking up late (what
luxury) and opening
presents and celebrating
Christmas quietly – hope
you have a lovely
Christmas

❦❦

love
Rolf

ROLF HARRIS

To children
everywhere
MERRY XMAS

PAUL NICHOLAS

❦❦ HAPPY CHRISTMAS
TO CHILDLINE,
PEACE ON EARTH AND
GOODWILL TO ALL KIDS.
INCLUDING MINE. ❦❦

Love Paul Nicholas
xxx

PAUL NICHOLAS

POSY SIMMONDS

Merry Chrishmassh!

COLIN HAWKINS

Colin Hawkins

❦❦ SEASONS GREETINGS TO
CHILDLINE
I shall spend the early
part of Christmas Day
submerged by the
wrapping paper from
(mostly other people's)
presents and most of the
rest of the day in a
euphoric haze brought on
by goodwill and claret. ❦❦

MICHAEL ASPEL

❦❦ HERE'S HOPING THAT YOU
WILL BE SPENDING
CHRISTMAS AS I WILL,
SURROUNDED BY THOSE YOU
LOVE AND CARE ABOUT. ❦❦

LESLIE GRANTHAM *"Dirty Den"*

❦❦ I'M SORRY I CAN'T DRAW BUT
HAPPY CHRISTMAS AND
THANKS FOR YOUR GOOD
WORK. ❦❦

EDWINA CURRIE

Hi Gang!

Colin Hawkins 1987.

Anne x

Maureen x

The Nolans wish you

Coleen x

Bernie xxx

🍃🍃 A MERRY CHRISTMAS AND A

HAPPY NEW YEAR.

LOTS OF LOVE

Christmas has always

been a very special time

of year for The Nolans.

The whole family get

together and, as you can

imagine, the house is

bedlam. But this is all

part of the fun. It's a

wonderful, happy time

that we look forward to

all year round. 🍃🍃

Lots of Love
"The Nolan's"
xxxx.

THE NOLANS

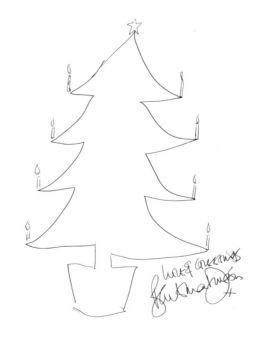

With Greetings
Barbara Dickson

BARBARA DICKSON

🍃🍃 TO ALL AT CHILDLINE LOVE

AND GREETINGS 🍃🍃

Barbara Dickson x

BARBARA DICKSON

A HAPPY CHRISTMAS TO EVERYONE.

On Christmas Day, <u>always</u> stockings, no matter how old you are – Church with carols, home-made mince pies, candied fruit, nuts and dates, chestnut stuffing (no meat for me!). Brandy butter, thousands of sprouts, holly on the pictures, ginger wine and dry sherry, a brisk walk, a light supper, the Queen's speech, telephoning far away family, gloating over presents, a thank you letter list, food and water for the birds, new books to read, logs on the fire and wishing on a star.

JOANNA LUMLEY

JOANNA LUMLEY

ROBIN COUSINS

SKATING ALONG…
TO WISH YOU A VERY HAPPY
CHRISTMAS AND JOYFUL
NEW YEAR…

ROBIN COUSINS

IAN BECK

Most people's christmases
are sad

But thanks to Childline
it can be

Very glad

with love
Susan Hampshire

The publishers would like to thank the following for their kind help in putting this book together: SHARON MARTIN, MARINA MAHER, NICK BUTTERWORTH, VICTORIA WOLCOUGH AT CHRISTIES, SARAH CAPLIN, KIM HOWARTH, KERRY DALTON AND THE CHILDWATCH PRODUCTION TEAM.

The following companies gave their services free. The quality of this book is a tribute to them: TRICKETT & WEBB (DESIGN) GORDON FRAZER LTD, GINA SUSSENS ASSOCIATES, CHRISTIES, CHESTNUT PHOTOTYPESETTING LTD, MARTIN RETAIL GROUP, DOT GRADATIONS LTD (TEXT ORIGINATION), SLEEVEPRINT, BEDFORD (COVER ORIGINATION AND PRINTING), WILLIAM COLLINS SONS & CO LTD (TEXT PRINTING AND BINDING), TOWNSEND HOOK LTD (TEXT PAPER), IGGESAND CONVERTERS LTD (COVER BOARD), PROFILE (TRANSPARENCIES).

And lastly, a big thank you to all the artists and celebrities who spared the time and thought.